A ROOKIE READER®

I AM AN EXPLORER

By Amy Moses

Illustrations by Rick Hackney

Prepared under the direction of Robert Hillerich, Ph.D.

$10.95

1/96

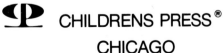

CHILDRENS PRESS®
CHICAGO

This book is dedicated to Miriam, Noah,
Joshua, Heidi, Celia, Cam, Scott, Emily, and Leo
because I have learned so much from you.

Library of Congress Cataloging-in-Publication Data

Moses, Amy I.
 I am an explorer / by Amy I. Moses
  p. cm. — (A Rookie reader)
 Summary: During a trip to the park, a child explores
an imaginary cave, mountain, jungle, and desert.
 ISBN 0-516-02059-5
 1. Explorers—Fiction. I. Title. II. Series.
PZ7.M84698Iam 1990
[E]—dc20   90-38374
                                                CIP
                                                AC

I am an explorer.

I'm off to see the world.

Up the mountain.

Down the mountain.

Into the cave.

Out of the cave.

Above the water.

Under the water.

Up the tree.

Down the tree.

Into the jungle.

Out of the jungle.

Above the ground.

Under the ground.

Up the stream.

Down the stream.

Into the desert.

Out of the desert.

Above the world.

Under the world.

Time to go home.

I am an explorer.

30 I have seen the world.

Tomorrow I'll explore outer space.

WORD LIST

above	ground	of	to
am	have	off	tomorrow
an	home	out	tree
cave	I	outer space	under
desert	I'll	see	up
down	I'm	seen	water
explore	into	stream	world
explorer	jungle	the	
go	mountain	time	

About the Author

When **Amy Moses** was growing up, her mother often said, "There's no reason to be bored." That comment inspired her and her sisters to make up imaginary worlds in which they could perform extraordinary feats. Having a vivid imagination has helped her in her careers as a teacher and a writer.

About the Artist

Richard Hackney is a San Francisco illustrator and writer who graduated from Art Center School in Los Angeles, California. He has worked at Disney Studios, drawn a syndicated comic strip, and has been an art director in advertising. He has also done some acting, written children's stories, and currently is doing a lot of educational illustration.

Richard lives with his wife, Elizabeth, and a black cat in a home on the edge of San Francisco Bay.